WAR
OVER THE WORD

by
Joe McIntyre

WAR OVER THE WORD

Published by
Empowering Grace Ministries
18706 N. Creek Pkwy., Suite 104
Bothell, WA 98011
Email: *joe_mcintyre@msn.com*

Capitalization: Joe McIntyre has taken *Author's Prerogative* in capitalizing certain words that are not usually capitalized according to standard grammatical practice. This is done for the purpose of clarity and emphasis.

Unless otherwise noted, all Scripture quotations are from the New King James Version of the Bible. Copyright © 1979, 1980, 1982 by Thomas Nelson Inc., publishers. Used by permission.

ISBN: 978-0-9778338-2-5

Printed in the United States by Morris Publishing
3212 East Highway 30
Kearney, NE 68847
1-800-650-7888

DEDICATION

I would like to dedicate this book to the wonderful body of believers at Word of His Grace Church and Ministry Center. Their love and support has been a great encouragement to me. I also want to voice my appreciation for the Leadership Team at WOHG. You are a great team and I thank the Lord for you.

ACKNOWLEDGMENTS

I would like to thank my assistant Linda Boone for all her help on preparing this book for publication. She is a wonder! I would also like to thank Marilyn Ratto for editing the manuscript and May Ridaliste who did the beautiful cover. Great job, May! Many thanks to the many people who have consistently prayed for me. You are really appreciated.

CONTENTS

INTRODUCTION

Some years ago, I heard a man teaching on the radio about the Parable of the Sower. He offered a series of tapes to further dig into the subject. I ordered the tapes and they proved to be life-changing for me. As I have taught on this parable over the years the response has been similar to my own response. Lights go on and people find clarity in their walk with the Lord where before things were foggy.

How do we grow spiritually? Why and how do Satan and demon forces attack us? Where do trials come from? How do we protect our hearts and become fruitful? What is the foundational parable of the kingdom?

All these questions and many others were answered for me as I came to understand Jesus' teaching in the Parable of the Sower. I had thought the parable was just about the lost hearing the Gospel. I didn't see the Kingdom principles contained in the teaching. I didn't see that Jesus was giving us the key to understanding the warfare in our lives. I didn't understand that He was showing us how to recognize and overcome the enemy's subtle assaults and bring forth fruit.

It all began in the Garden of Eden. When God spoke, He released the Kingdom Seed of His Holy Word. It had within it the Divine Potential to empower Adam and Eve to expand the Rule of God to the rest of the world. "Let them have dominion.." was both the command and the commission. Satan knew that if Adam and Eve placed themselves under the dominion of the Word, they would lack nothing necessary to accomplish it and thus overrule Satan's kingdom.

So his approach was, "Has God said?"

Getting Adam and Eve to doubt the authority of God's Word would both bring them into disobedience and bring them under Satan's domination. That War is still going on in every human life – believer or unbeliever. When we hear the Word and submit to it, the ability of God released by Him when He spoke becomes available to us. Coming under the authority of God's Word both protects and empowers us. The War is little understood by most believers.

Our destiny is to win this war.

Join me as we look into this parable and draw forth some of its riches.

Mark 4:3-20

3 "Listen! Behold, a sower went out to sow.

4 And it happened, as he sowed, that some seed fell by the wayside; and the birds of the air came and devoured it.

5 Some fell on stony ground, where it did not have much earth; and immediately it sprang up because it had no depth of earth.

6 But when the sun was up it was scorched, and because it had no root it withered away.

7 And some seed fell among thorns; and the thorns grew up and choked it, and it yielded no crop.

8 But other seed fell on good ground and yielded a crop that sprang up, increased and produced: some thirtyfold, some sixty, and some a hundred."

9 And He said to them, "He who has ears to hear, let him hear!"

10 But when He was alone, those around Him with the twelve asked Him about the parable.

11 And He said to them, "To you it has been given to know the mystery of the kingdom of God; but to those who are outside, all things come in parables,

12 so that 'Seeing they may see and not perceive, and hearing they may hear and not understand; Lest they should turn, and their sins be forgiven them.'" ["So that I should heal them"(Mt. 13:15)]

13 And He said to them, "Do you not understand this parable? How then will you understand all the parables?

14 The sower sows the word.

15 And these are the ones by the wayside where the word is sown. When they hear, Satan comes immediately and takes away the word that was sown in their hearts.

16 These likewise are the ones sown on stony ground who, when they hear the word, immediately receive it with gladness;

17 and they have no root in themselves, and so endure only for a time. Afterward, when tribulation or persecution arises for the word's sake, immediately they stumble.

18 Now these are the ones sown among thorns; they are the ones who hear the word,

19 and the cares of this world, the deceitfulness of riches, and the desires for other things entering in choke the word, and it becomes unfruitful.

20 But these are the ones sown on good ground, those who hear the word, accept it, and bear fruit: some thirtyfold, some sixty, and some a hundred."

Chapter One

THE PARABLE

Most of us have heard this parable and understood its application to the lost. When they hear the gospel Satan comes and seeks to steal the Word from them before they can act on it and be saved. The parable shows us the things Satan uses to steal the Word: Satanic attack, persecution, affliction, cares of this world, desire for other things and the deceitfulness of riches. Most of us grasp how Satan uses these weapons against the unbeliever when he or she hears the gospel preached.

But notice that the Word brings forth thirty, sixty and a hundredfold. The parable is certainly true concerning the unbeliever, but the same principles apply to the believer in the war over the Word in our lives. Satan uses the same type of barrage to steal the Word from our hearts as he does with the unbeliever. If we are ignorant of this truth, we are ill-equipped to spot and overcome his attacks.

To really benefit from this book, it would be good to spend some time pouring over the parable and its interpretation. Familiarize yourself with the various soils and the things that are used to steal the Word. Remember, the point is how the Word can bring forth fruit in our lives and what we must do to allow it to do so.

All progress in the Christian life is by God's Word. Peter writes, "…desire the sincere milk of the Word, that you may grow thereby"(1 Pet. 2: 2). It is the creative and sustaining virtue of the Scriptures that causes us to grow in the grace of God. The war is over the Word.

What does this mean?

The Written Word

First of all, the war is over the written Word of God. We are made partakers of the divine nature through the promises of God (2 Pet. 1:3,4). Our human spirit was created to feed upon God's Word which is "spirit and life" (John 6:63). All the promises of God are "Yes and Amen" to us in Christ (2 Cor. 1:20). Every need we would ever face in life has been foreseen and provided for in the promises of the Word. In the Old Covenant their inheritance was a Promised Land. In the New Covenant our inheritance is a Land of Promises. Every provision is in the promises.

The Quickened Word

Many times as we prayerfully study the Scriptures, the Holy Spirit seems to underline and embolden certain passages of the Word to us. These promises take on a deeper significance to us and encourage our faith profoundly. Father makes His Word to be His voice to us. In a way we might not be able to articulate, we know intuitively that the quickened promise is our Father's Word to us. One of the fruits of prayerful study - or meditation - in the Word is that we give the Holy Spirit an opportunity to quicken (or make alive) God's written Word to us. This imparts faith and compels action. As we act on the Word, God acts on our behalf.

The Prophetic Word

Another way God speaks to us, and therefore another place of application of this parable, is the prophetic Word. God speaks to

10

us as people prophesy over us. Every prophetic Word will be contested by the enemy. He will try to steal it from our hearts.

> **Matthew 4:4**
> But He answered and said, "It is written, 'Man shall not live by bread alone, but by **every word** that proceeds from the mouth of God.'"

God will often speak words to us about our destiny and calling, confirming what we are perceiving in our spirit concerning God's will for our life, or a direction we should take. Our obedience brings blessing, therefore it will be challenged by the enemy.

Dreams, Visions and Other Signs

In the prophetic books, we find phrases like "The Word of the Lord came to so-and-so in a vision, or in a dream.." Though the form may vary, God is still communicating His Word to us even in visions and dreams. They are creative Seed sown in the inner man for the purpose of creating faith and obedience resulting in blessing and the furtherance of God's Kingdom purpose. Therefore the same principle of the Sower applies to them as well. Satan will come to distract and divert us from allowing the Word of the Lord to bring forth the God-intended fruit.

The Words We Speak

As a people in whom dwells the Holy Spirit, the potential power released in our words is not always understood and appreciated. As a person created in the image and likeness of God, your words - under the leadership of the Spirit - can release God's creative ability. Our words carry authority whether we understand it or not. We will be judged for every idle word we speak.

Matthew 12:36
But I say to you that for **every idle word** men may speak, they will give account of it in the day of judgment.

If my words were powerless and carried no substance, why would I have to give an account of them on the Day of Judgment? Since the primary way spiritual authority is released is by the words of our mouth, there is warfare over what we say. Satan knows if we learn to use our words wisely and creatively, it will lead to his defeat.

Revelation 12:11
And they overcame him by the blood of the Lamb and by **the word of their testimony**.

Our words can cause us to overcome Satan or succumb to him. Words of doubt, fear and unbelief open the door to his oppression. Words of faith, courage and love draw the presence of God and subdue dark forces. When we fill our words with His Word and constantly speak of His goodness and His faithfulness, we are encouraged and so are those who hear us. There is war over us getting His Word on our lips and speaking in line with His promises.

Job 22:2 NASU
You will also decree a thing, and it will be established for you; And light will shine on your ways.

The war is over the Word.

Chapter Two

THE WORD

One of the weaknesses of the modern Church is a failure to appreciate the authority of God's Word. The Bible is viewed as a great source for sound doctrine (which it is!) but not as a practical handbook for successful living. The first move of many believers when they face a crisis is not "What does God's Word say about my problem?" but rather "Who can I call to help me?"

We do need one another. And we need pastoral ministries to stand with us during challenging times. But the maturing believer wants to know what Father has said about the problem before he consults with man. One of the great helps to us in trials is getting those around us to agree with us on a promise from the Word. We bring our instability and frailty into agreement with the unchanging, unshakeable Word of God.

As our walk with the Lord Jesus matures, He introduces us to His Father. As we learn to abide in the Father's love and acceptance, the written Word becomes His voice to us. He causes His Word to answer all our questions. We enter into a dialogue with heaven where He leads us by reminding us of promises and statements in His Word that deal with our area of difficulty. There is a promise (if not *many* promises) that deals with every area of life and all its challenges.

13

Incorruptible Seed

1 Peter 1:23
Having been born again, not of corruptible seed but incorruptible, through the word of God which lives and abides forever...

God's Word is incorruptible Seed. The Word of God is sown in your heart, and if it is not stolen by the enemy, it will bring forth after its own kind. The divine nature is contained in the incorruptible Seed (2 Pet. 1:4). When we hear the Word with our inner man (not just our intellect) it begins a creative work in us. We receive with meekness the implanted Word and it brings God's salvation to whatever area of our lives we need it (James 1:21).

If you think about seed, corn seed, for example, all the potential for a crop of corn is contained in the seed. If it can successfully be put in the ground, watered and cared for, the outcome will be a crop of corn. But with natural seed, sometimes the seed is bad and it will fail to bring forth. It might be corrupt.

God's Word is incorruptible Seed. If we protect and water it, it is guaranteed to bring forth the specified crop. Whatever the Word promises is what the seed will bring forth. The principle is so simple that a child could understand it. Yet that doesn't mean that the war over the Word won't be vicious. When we understand what the war is really about we are much better equipped to be victorious in the warfare.

The apostle Paul illustrates this in First Corinthians:

1 Corinthians 3:5-7
5 Who then is Paul, and who is Apollos, but ministers through whom you believed, as the Lord gave to each one?
6 I planted, Apollos watered, but God gave the increase.
7 So then neither he who plants is anything, nor he who waters, but God who gives the increase.

14

Paul had planted the Incorruptible Seed, Apollos had then come and watered it. But because what they were planting and watering was the Incorruptible Seed of God's Word, God Himself gave the increase. Every time we take in the Word of God, the potential for spiritual development is present. Father watches over His Word to perform it (Jer. 1:12).

Alive and Powerful

God's Word is His nature expressed. There's Divine Life in the Word. There's power in the Word. Hebrews says:

> **Hebrews 4:12**
> For the word of God is living and powerful, and sharper than any two-edged sword, piercing even to the division of soul and spirit, and of joints and marrow, and is a discerner of the thoughts and intents of the heart.

The Word is living and powerful. Peter told us it lives and abides forever. We are handling a book with Divine Life in it. "The Words I speak," Jesus said, "are spirit and they are Life" (Jn. 6:63). There is spiritual power in the Word. But like a natural seed, we never see the potential brought forth until it is put in the right environment and properly cared for. The heart of man is the proper environment for the seed to germinate. Merely having it in our intellects does not release the seed's potential. It must make its way into our inner man, the hidden man of the heart. Not the mind only, but the deeper place of our human consciousness.

It Accomplishes God's Purpose

All the potential for accomplishing God's purpose is contained in His promises and the declarations in the Word. The Word is the agent for bringing to pass what He desires in the earth.

15

Isaiah 55:11
So shall My word be that goes forth from My mouth; It shall not return to Me void,
But it shall accomplish what I please, and it shall prosper in the thing for which I sent it.

Every Word God speaks has within it the power to accomplish what it says. God expects His Word to be fruitful and He never says anything frivolously. Every declaration of God is throbbing with Life. A low view of the Word will cripple its effectiveness in our lives. We must come to value the Word the way God values it. "Can two walk together unless they agree?" (Amos 3:3).

Many believers are looking everywhere in desperation for spiritual help. It never occurs to them that they have devalued the Word and therefore are not skillful in appropriating the promises. Their thought is "Oh, I believe the Bible, but I need help with my problems." They substitute mental assent to the Scriptures for a real heart faith in God's Word.

We Live By the Word

When Jesus was tempted, He defeated the devil by quoting the Word. "It is written" was his method. His Father's Word was in His heart and He defeated the devil by the power in the incorruptible Seed. He didn't use His power as deity. He didn't say, "I'm the Messiah, devil, you can't mess with Me." He knew and used the authority of His covenant with God and relied on the resident power in the declaration of Scripture.

Matthew 4:4
But He answered and said, "It is written, 'Man shall not live by bread alone, but by every word that proceeds from the mouth of God.'"

In defeating the enemy, He indicated that the secret to victory was an intimate relationship with the words that proceed from the mouth of God. Anyone serious about victory will become a good student of God's Word. "Your Word have I hidden in my heart, that I might not sin against You" (Ps. 119:11). The Psalmist understood the power and life in the Word.

The Word Produces Fruit

The natural outcome of seed planted and cared for is fruit. We all want to be fruitful in our lives. We want the fruit of the Spirit to abound in our walk with the Lord. *Fruit comes from seed!* As we learn to protect and nurture the seed of God's Word in our hearts, we are guaranteed that it will bring forth fruit: some thirty, some sixty, some a hundredfold.

Speaking of the power of the Gospel, Paul writes:

Colossians 1:6
...which has come to you, as it has also in all the world, and **is bringing forth fruit**, as it is also among you since the day you heard and knew the grace of God in truth...

All the potential is in the Seed! Notice that the Word brought forth fruit in them when they knew the grace of God in truth. They stopped struggling in the flesh and let the Word work in them. The inherent power of the Word freely given to us is the grace of God in manifestation.

Paul describes the working of the Word when affirming the Thessalonians.

1 Thessalonians 2:13
For this reason we also thank God without ceasing, because when you received the word of God which you heard from us, you welcomed it not as the word of men, but as it is in truth, the word of God, which also **effectively works in you who believe.**

17

Paul uses a word in this verse (Gk. *Energeo*) for *effectively works* from which we get our English word *energy*. Thayer's Lexicon suggests "to be operative, be at work, put forth power," as meanings for the word. Contained within the Seed of God's Word is His divine energy. Power to walk in the Spirit, to overcome the world and to walk and live by faith is all contained within the incorruptible Seed of God's Living Word.

The key to fruitfulness is learning how to cooperate with the Word until it brings forth its fruit in us. We must cultivate a high view of the power and authority of the written Word of God. As we do, we begin to "receive with meekness the implanted Word" (James 1:21). The prophet Isaiah also talks about a company of God's people that will draw His attention.

> **Isaiah 66:2b**
> But on this one will I look: On him who is poor and of a contrite spirit, and who trembles at My word.

The ones that Isaiah describes have a deep reverence for the Word of God. They "tremble" at the Word. They reverence and honor the Word like they would God Himself. And note that these are the ones to whom God's attention will be given.

If there has been in you any attitude that has failed to honor God's Word and reverence it, now might be a good time to ask forgiveness and make a fresh commitment to esteem the Word as God would have you esteem it.

> **Hebrews 3:12**
> Beware, brethren, lest there be in any of you **an evil heart of unbelief** in departing from the living God...

Unbelief is the subtlest of sins. It is hardly recognized as sin by much of the Church. Yet, here it is constituted as an *evil heart.* That's serious. What does the writer mean by unbelief? A few verses later he answers that question.

Hebrews 4:2
For indeed the gospel was preached to us as well as to them; but **the word which they heard did not profit them, not being mixed with faith in those who heard it.**

Their attitude toward the Word disqualified them from entering into the Promised Land. Do you think perhaps the same attitude could keep us from entering into our Land of Promises? Undoubtedly. My intention with this book is to help believers enter in and enjoy their inheritance. We are learning to possess the promises and let the promises possess us.

This is what the war is over. In the next chapter we will take a closer look at this war.

Chapter Three

WHY THE WAR?

Mark 4:15
And these are the ones by the wayside where the word is sown.
When they hear, Satan comes immediately and takes away the
word that was sown in their hearts.

The creative ability of God comes to us in Seed form in the
Word of God. Man's heart was designed to be the fertile ground
in which the Living Word would take root and bring forth fruit.
All the potential for a changed life is in the Seed. We become
partakers of the divine nature through these powerful promises (2
Pet. 1:4). We encounter the Living Word through the written
Word.

1 Corinthians 3:6 NIV
I planted the seed, Apollos watered it, but God made it grow.

One can plant, and another can water the Word in our lives. In
fact, we can plant and water the Word in our lives. But God, and
only God can give the increase. The life is in the Seed. We can
learn to guard the process of sowing and watering, trusting our
Father to be faithful to grant the increase.

So why the warfare? Why does Satan bitterly attack the
believer when he hears the Word? In this chapter I want us to
consider some reasons why he fears the power and anointing on
the Word.

20

The Word Reveals God

Every bit of truth that you know about God has come through the written Word of God. Even if you have had a personal visitation from the Lord, you judged its validity by how much it agreed with the written Word. The only accurate revelation of the nature and character of God is the Scriptures. When you were unsaved, you likely had many misconceptions concerning God.

After we come to know the Lord we begin the process of renewing our minds. Part of that renewal involves developing a true and accurate image of God. We begin the process of shedding the misconceptions and wrong concepts we have held of God and His attitude toward us.

Satan uses our misconceptions regarding the Lord to cause us to retreat from our Father and fall under a cloud of condemnation. Though the Word says there is no condemnation in Christ (Rom. 8:1), a wrong image of God causes us to think He gets angry with us every time we fail. Satan "shames" us and we draw back from the only Source of help adequate to deal with our weaknesses. The Word says we can come boldly to the throne of grace and obtain mercy (Heb. 4:16). When you sin, you need mercy. Mercy is constantly being offered to us and the moment we acknowledge our sin we can obtain His mercy.

The written Word progressively unveils Him who is the Living Word. The Holy Spirit takes the things of Jesus and reveals them to us. He guides us into all Truth. The Truth makes us free (Jn. 8:32). Jesus came to bring the true revelation of the Father into the midst of many religious ideas. The greater our revelation of the true character and nature of our Father, the more we enter into rest and into effective, fruitful prayer and victorious Christian living. Our confidence in Father and His Word grows by leaps and bounds. Our faith begins to bring Father much pleasure (Heb. 10:38; 11:6).

The written Word reveals the Living Word. The Living Word is the perfect revelation of the Father. As we come to know the

21

Father and the Son in Truth, our Christian walk stabilizes. We become established in the grace of God.

The Word Creates Faith in God

The Word is God's agent for creating faith in us. "Faith comes by hearing, hearing by the Word of God" (Rom. 10:17). Faith flows from the heart of the Father through the Word of God into our hearts. Without faith it is impossible to please God, so Father has made the way for us to continually grow in faith. One scholar defines faith as "the leaning of the entire human personality upon God or the Messiah in absolute trust and confidence in His power, goodness and wisdom."[1] We will only do this if we see Him accurately. The good news is the ability to see Him accurately comes to us as Father unveils His Word to us. Our unlimited faith potential is in the incorruptible Seed of God's Word.

As we learn to humble ourselves and reverence the written Word of God, the Holy Spirit causes it to become for us the Living, Faith-imparting Word. Our hearts are flooded with loving trust in our heavenly Father and the Lord Jesus Christ. Faith comes by hearing, hearing by the Word of God.

Faith on the human side, involves a decision to believe. We must choose to believe. Although we can't "work up" faith, we still must choose to believe before the Holy Spirit will quicken the Word. We come to God with His promises and the statements of fact from His Word and we say, "Father, this is what You have said. I put myself in agreement with it. No Word You speak is void of power (Luke 1:37 ASV). I receive in meekness Your implanted Word (James 1:21). I choose to believe."

Our choice invites the Father to impart faith to our hearts.

---

[1] *A Pocket Lexicon to the Greek New Testament,* Alexander Souter, (Oxford, at the Clarendon Press, 1949) p.203, *pistis.*

Hebrews 4:2
For indeed the gospel was preached to us as well as to them; but the word which they heard did not profit them, not being mixed with faith in those who heard it.

Our choice to believe the Word of God "mixes" faith with the Word and the Word begins to profit us.

Faith Makes God's Power Available

Matthew 19:26
But Jesus looked at them and said to them, "With men this is impossible, but with God all things are possible."

With God all things are possible. We all believe this to be true. But what about the corollary?

Mark 9:23
Jesus said to him, "If you can believe, all things are possible to him who believes."

Jesus here says the same unlimited power of God is opened up to the believer. Through faith we can become channels of God's omnipotence. Faith allows His limitlessness to flow through our lives into this world. You can see why Satan would fear our developing faith. Our faith invites God to release His unbridled power through us into this world. Satan is no match for God's power. Therefore, Satan is no match for the believer who learns how to develop his faith and becomes the channel of God's power in the earth.

Satan is Overcome by Faith

1 John 5:4
For whatever is born of God overcomes the world. And this is the victory that has overcome the world - our faith.

1 John 2:14b NIV
I write to you, young men, because you are strong, and the word of God lives in you, and you have overcome the evil one.

Our maturing faith gives us victory over the influence of this world. Many believers become entangled in the affairs of this life. They are stressed out and weighed down with anxiety. Strong faith will cause us to overcome the world's influences. Our adversary is seeking those whose faith is weak so he can devour them with the anxieties of life.

1 Peter 5:8-9
8 Be sober, be vigilant; because your adversary the devil walks about like a roaring lion, seeking whom he may devour.
9 Resist him, steadfast in your faith, knowing that the same sufferings are experienced by your brotherhood in the world.

Notice in the above passage that it is a steadfast (strong, enduring) faith that stands and resists the devil. He seeks to devour us but our confidence in our Father and His faithfulness cannot be shaken. We trust Him with all our hearts and we lean not to our own understanding (Prov. 3:5). We learn to put on the whole armor of God and fight the good fight of faith. It's a good fight because we are guaranteed to win if we don't faint (Gal. 6:9).

All of God's Provisions are Available to Faith

As good spiritual "farmers" we are learning to plant the Seed of God's promises and care for them until they bring forth "after their own kind."

Genesis 1:12
And the earth brought forth grass, the herb that yields seed according to its kind, and the tree that yields fruit, whose seed is in itself according to its kind. And God saw that it was good.

The reproductive cycle of seed that brings forth after its own kind was part of the original creation. We find the law of sowing and reaping from Genesis to Revelation. We are good ground designed by Father to bring forth abundantly. He has provided the Incorruptible Seed. Our part is to hear it and protect it. Once we understand what the war is really about, we can intelligently cooperate with Father. We stop striving in our own strength and trust in the latent power in the Seed.

Luke 8:12
Those by the wayside are the ones who hear; then the devil comes and takes away the word out of their hearts, lest they should believe and be saved.

This parable is often applied to the lost because it talks about believing and being saved. And it certainly is applicable to the lost. But it is important to understand the Bible meaning of "saved" is much broader than the New Birth. *Saved* in the Bible means *deliverance* in almost any form it might be needed. Our salvation is both instantaneous and progressive. Our spirit has been saved, our souls are being saved. Our bodies may experience a measure of God's saving power in healing us and keeping us well. Ultimately the fullness of our salvation will come and we will receive a new body. All the promises of God define the total concept of our salvation.

We obtain every aspect of our salvation by faith. As we gain clarity from God's Word about the things He is offering us in the promises, we begin to receive them by faith. As surely as we were Born Again by faith, we receive the Holy Spirit by faith, healing is received by faith, sanctification can be received by faith, financial provision comes by faith. The list is endless. All the promises of God are "Yes and Amen" in Christ (2 Cor. 1:20).

Satan fears your developing faith. Every believer can develop strong faith. Faith causes you to overcome Satan and accomplish the Father's will. You extend the Kingdom as you release His authority in the earth. Satan will do all he can to short-circuit your development of faith. That's what the war is over. But God has made you good ground and is teaching you how to sow and how to reap.

James 4:7
Therefore submit to God. Resist the devil and he will flee from you.

As we submit ourselves to God - and to the expression of His divine nature, His Word - we are empowered to effectively resist the devil. The sword of the Spirit which is the Word of God is God's flaming Sword of Vengeance to the enemy. He will flee from the believer who is submitted to God and His Word. Our declaration of the Word is a higher authority than Satan can wield. He must flee. God and you are a majority.

Chapter Four

EARS TO HEAR

Mark 4:9
And He said to them, "He who has ears to hear, let him hear!"

Jesus knew every one listening to Him had ears on their heads. He knew they all heard and recognized the words He was using. But what He was obviously talking about was a kind of hearing that impacted the life of the hearer in a deep way. In another place He said:

Luke 9:44
"Let these words sink down into your ears…"

Jesus wanted His disciples to fully grasp what He was saying. He wanted the Truth to set them free. He wants the same for you and me. He wants the Incorruptible Word to so take root in our hearts that it becomes a part of us. We conform our thoughts to His thoughts. We think like sons of God instead of sons of Adam.

This can only happen if we learn the art of stewarding the revelation God gives us. Satan fears our gaining revelation and applying it effectively to our lives. That will spell his defeat. So we must learn to protect the Word sown in our hearts.

27

A Decision

We cannot be passive hearers and expect the Word to do its job. We must make a decision to believe and make the Word our own.

Mark 4:20
But these are the ones sown on good ground, those who hear the word, **accept it**, and bear fruit: some thirtyfold, some sixty, and some a hundred.

Notice that the "good ground" people hear the Word *and accept it.* They make a decision to possess the Word, to contend for it if necessary. The Amplified Bible says they 'receive, accept and welcome it.' Perceiving the authority of the Word of the Lord, they decide to take it to themselves and refuse to be passive. The Christian life is not lived in will power, but God will do little in our lives until we make a decision. Our will is very important.

Understanding

In Matthew's version of the parable, he adds an interesting word.

Matthew 13:23
But he who received seed on the good ground is he who hears the word and **understands it**, who indeed bears fruit and produces: some a hundredfold, some sixty, some thirty."

Compare this with the 19th verse:

Matthew 13:19
When anyone hears the word of the kingdom, and **does not understand it**, then the wicked one comes and snatches away what was sown in his heart. This is he who received seed by the wayside.

28

There is an incubation time of the Word. A digesting time. After the initial hearing, as we watch over the Word in our hearts, God will bring understanding to us so we can practically apply the Truth to our lives. It is during this time - between hearing and understanding - that Satan attempts to steal the Word from us.

The Greek word for *understanding* means to "put it together, like the pieces in a jigsaw puzzle." When we first hear a new and exciting Word, we "receive it with gladness" (Mk. 4:16). But that is only the beginning. The Holy Spirit wants to take that Word and show us how to make it workable in our lives. He intends to show us how to bring forth fruit. He wants to give us *revelation*.

Cultivation

It takes time to allow the Spirit to teach us the application of Truth. We must hold the Word before the Lord in a teachable posture, expecting Him to bring Light on His Word. We learn to quietly contemplate the meaning of the Word and let it impact our inner man. Intellectual knowledge doesn't change lives. Revelation knowledge does.

God instructed Joshua at a strategic time in his life, what to do to guarantee wise decisions:

Joshua 1:8
This Book of the Law shall not depart from your mouth, but you shall meditate in it day and night, that you may observe to do according to all that is written in it. For then you will make your way prosperous, and then you will have good success.

Notice that the Hebrew form of meditation involved not letting the Word depart from his *mouth*. Hebrews who practiced Scripture meditation continually spoke the Word while contemplating the meaning and application to the problems of

29

life. It was a devotional exercise, not merely a mechanical one. Some today call it "pray-reading" the Scriptures.

Whatever we call it, it gets the Word off the page and into our heart. It allows the Spirit time to unveil the heart behind each promise. Every Scripture is a revelation of God Himself. The promises and declarations of the Word are given to reveal our God to us. The Christian life is a progressive unveiling of the greatness and goodness of our God. The more we know Him, the more we change. The promises are the means, knowing Him is the end.

Guarding the Word

Luke 8:15
But the ones that fell on the good ground are those who, having heard the word with a noble and good heart, **keep it** and bear fruit with patience.

Recognizing the great potential in the Word, we also recognize Satan's attempts to steal it. We make up our minds - with God's grace - to refuse to let it be stolen. At this point in the process many believers are shocked to see how vicious the attacks of the enemy really are! Now that we understand what the war is over, we are not mystified by what happens, but often it dawns on believers in a new way, how serious Satan is about stopping the Word. He is a creature of fear, who knows his days are numbered. Believers who begin to learn how to draw God's power and grace into their lives are a continual threat to him.

Study, meditate, pray and declare the Word. Don't let it depart from your eyes (Prov. 4:20, 21). Satan will attempt through people and circumstances to distract you and get you side-tracked. Recognize and resist these attempts. Rebuke his forces. Resist the devil and he will flee from you (James 4:7).

Steadfast Faith

Initial faith comes at the moment of illumination by the Spirit. Steadfast faith is developed in the trial of your faith.

James 1:2-3
2 My brethren, count it all joy when you fall into various trials,
3 knowing that **the testing of your faith** produces patience.

When our faith is tested, there is a promise of it developing something valuable in us. Our English word *patience* is actually way too weak a word for the Greek concept. This word is a militant term, implying courage and unswerving loyalty. It is used as in the courage of a stout-hearted soldier who never leaves his post and endures until the battle is over.

Your faith has the potential of developing in you this kind of character. The apostle Paul uses this same word in Romans.

Romans 5:3-4
3 And not only that, but we also glory in tribulations, knowing that tribulation produces **perseverance**;
4 and **perseverance**, character; and character, hope.

Paul states it a little differently, but makes the same point. Our tribulations - the testing of our faith - produces, he says, perseverance. The word translated *perseverance* is the same word translated *patience* in James 1:3. This perseverance which is developed in the fiery trials of our faith produces character. Learning to stand against all the assault of the enemy to steal the Word, develops not only perseverance, but also develops our character. And, Paul goes on to say, character results in hope.

Bible hope is a much stronger term than the way we commonly use it. We say, "I hope I get that job." We mean it would be nice, but we don't actually have much confidence that it will happen. When the Bible speaks of hope it is talking about something rooted in the character and faithfulness of God. It

31

looks to the future with expectancy because it knows the One in whom it is trusting. *Assurance* might be closer to the Biblical idea of hope.

Faith and Patience

As we understand the nature of the war we are in, we become good soldiers of Jesus Christ. We understand the war over the Word and we are no longer willing to let Satan steal the Word from us. Through faith and patience we are determined to let the Word bear fruit in our lives.

> **Hebrews 10:35-36**
> 35 Therefore do not cast away your confidence, which has great reward.
> 36 For you have need of **endurance**, so that after you have done the will of God, you may receive the promise...

The word translated *endurance* in the above verse is the same Greek word translated *patience* and *perseverance* in the previously mentioned verses. We all must develop this grace. Earlier in Hebrews it says:

> **Hebrews 6:12**
> that you do not become sluggish, but imitate those who through **faith** and **patience** inherit the promises.

Don't waste your trials by complaining and moaning. Rejoice, because what Satan meant to steal the Word is now producing in you the thing he fears: a strong, patient faith. It is also giving you the kind of victory that makes you face the future with true, Bible hope.

> **2 Timothy 2:3**
> You therefore must endure hardship as a good soldier of Jesus Christ.

32

Through faith and patience we can obtain the promises. Father promises to make all things ultimately serve His purpose no matter what was intended by the enemy. We face our future with the kind of confidence that only those who are learning to trust God and His Word can have.

Chapter Five

MIND STORMS

As we ponder this parable, we see that Satan uses a number of methods to attempt to steal the Word. It is our responsibility to stop the thief! It becomes much easier when we understand the methods he will use to uproot the Word from our hearts. In this and the next few chapters, we will examine the six methods Satan uses to steal the Word from the good ground of our inner man.

Mark 4:4
And it happened, as he sowed, that some seed fell by the wayside; and the birds of the air came and devoured it.

In the parable, the first soil mentioned is the wayside soil. Jesus says the birds of the air came and devoured the seed. Notice, now the interpretation of the verse:

Mark 4:15
And these are the ones by the wayside where the word is sown. When they hear, Satan comes immediately and takes away the word that was sown in their hearts.

As soon as you hear a message that could potentially change your life, or as you are reading the Word and the Spirit opens it up to you in a fresh way, you receive a personal word of

34

prophecy, or you make a declaration of your faith, Satan is going to come and attempt to remove the Word from your life.

Satan doesn't come personally, he sends his "birds" to do his work. Notice this verse from:

Revelation 18:1-2
1 After these things I saw another angel coming down from heaven, having great authority, and the earth was illuminated with his glory.
2 And he cried mightily with a loud voice, saying, "Babylon the great is fallen, is fallen, and has become a dwelling place of demons, a prison for **every foul spirit**, and a cage for **every unclean and hated bird!**

Birds are used here as a type for demonic spirits. Oppressing spirits come and speak to our minds with thoughts of doubt, fear and condemnation. It can be so subtle that you think it's your own thought. "Why am I thinking this," you wonder. Demons spirits bring their suggestions to your mind. These thoughts of doubt and unbelief are usually along the lines of our weaknesses as we walked in the Old Creation. We often hardly recognize them as the demonic weapon they are. They seek to undermine our faith in the Word.

The enemy wants us to be double-minded so that our faith never produces what was promised.

James 1:5-8
5 If any of you lacks wisdom, let him ask of God, who gives to all liberally and without reproach, and it will be given to him.
6 But let him ask in faith, with no doubting, for he who doubts is like a wave of the sea driven and tossed by the wind.
7 For let not that man suppose that he will receive anything from the Lord;
8 he is a double-minded man, unstable in all his ways.

As Satan attacks our minds with his "mind storms," we become double-minded and are removed from the position of receiving from God. For the Word to produce in us we must hold fast to it and not allow it to be stolen by the enemy.

The unrenewed mind seldom brings forth much fruit. We must renew our minds to be in agreement with our recreated spirit. Notice how Paul speaks of this in Romans:

Romans 8:5-7 Recovery Version
5 For those who are according to the flesh mind the things of the flesh; but those who are according to the spirit, the things of Spirit.
6 For the mind set on the flesh is death, but the mind set on the spirit is life and peace..

Your human spirit has been renewed and by nature it agrees with God. Your unrenewed mind, on the other hand, agrees with your flesh. As your mind is renewed it begins to agree with the Realities of the New Creation Life in your inner man and reject the strongholds of the Old Man.

Paul tells us of the need of a renewed mind in Romans 12. Our minds make great servants, but they are poor masters. As they are renewed they become an honorable servant to the inner man, the hidden man of the heart.

Romans 12:1-2
I beseech you therefore, brethren, by the mercies of God, that you present your bodies a living sacrifice, holy, acceptable to God, which is your reasonable service.
2 And do not be conformed to this world, but be transformed by the renewing of your mind, that you may prove what is that good and acceptable and perfect will of God.

Notice how Kenneth Wuest translates this verse:

36

Romans 12:2 (Wuest)
And stop assuming an outward expression that does not come from within you and is not representative of what you are in your inner being but is patterned after this age; but change your outward expression to one that comes from within and is representative of your inner being, by the renewing of your mind...

The New Creation man on the inside needs to teach and train the mind through the Word so that it is a fitting companion for the spirit. We learn to continually speak and meditate on the Words of Life that God gives us and we prevent Satan from stealing them. As we hold fast, the Word will bring forth 'after its own kind.'

There is a battle for your mind. The mind is the battlefield, the will is the prize. Satan wants you to choose, whether actively or passively, to give up on the Word of promise. Notice how Paul describes our battle:

2 Corinthians 10:3-5
3 For though we walk in the flesh, we do not war according to the flesh.
4 For the weapons of our warfare are not carnal but mighty in God for pulling down strongholds,
5 casting down arguments and every high thing that exalts itself against the knowledge of God, bringing every thought into captivity to the obedience of Christ...

The key concepts in this passage are *strongholds, arguments, high things* and *thoughts.* All of these have to do with the mind. This isn't talking about pulling down principalities and powers as some have suggested. It's talking about the strongholds in the mind that resist the Truth of God and hold to some form of unbelief. The weapons that God has given us are mighty to pull these things down and get them out of our minds. We erect new "strongholds" of Truth as our minds are renewed.

As we study the Word under the tutelage of the Spirit, as we boldly declare the promises and as we quietly meditate in the things the Spirit has given us in promise form, we pull down these mental strongholds and our minds become our allies in the fight of faith. We say, "Peace, be still" to the enemy's mind storms. You can defeat the enemy's attacks on your mind.

In the next chapter we will look at Satan's next weapon to steal the Word and how we may overcome it.

Chapter Six

THE PRESSURE OF CIRCUMSTANCES

In our last chapter we considered the first of Satan's attacks against us to steal the Word. He, by means of demon spirits, assaults our minds with doubt and unbelief. He attempts to focus us on our weaknesses and shortcomings. These "mind storms" are designed to get our focus off of protecting and nurturing the Word that we have heard. Our response is to learn to recognize and resist these attacks and to pursue the renewing of our minds.

As Jesus goes on in the Parable, he discusses another type of ground.

Mark 4:16-17
16 These likewise are the ones sown on stony ground who, when they hear the word, immediately receive it with gladness; 17 and they have no root in themselves, and so endure only for a time. Afterward, when **tribulation** or **persecution** arises for the word's sake, immediately they stumble.

Notice how Luke relates this verse:

Luke 8:13
13 But the ones on the rock are those who, when they hear, receive the word with joy; and these have no root, who believe for awhile and **in time of temptation** fall away.

Luke summarizes Mark's statement by calling it a "time of temptation." The Greek word translated *temptation* means to "put to some type of test." This would include temptation, but the word is broader than merely tempting. It might be translated *temptation, test or trial* and capture the full meaning.

Here we are confronted with a powerful truth: Our trials do not come from God, but rather from the Adversary to get the Word out of our hearts. It is widely taught that God is orchestrating our trials to teach us. Remember, Jesus is the perfect Unveiler of the Father. He says it is Satan that comes with tests and trials, not to perfect our faith, but rather to destroy it.

Many believers walk in a sort of "Twilight Zone" of confusion about who is orchestrating the trials in their lives. Unsure whether God or the Devil is behind the trial they remain passive and try to figure out what they are supposed to learn from the trial. *God must have allowed this for a purpose*, they reason. What if God had nothing to do with the trial and it was, as Jesus said, designed by Satan to steal the Word? We are told in the Word to resist the Devil and he will flee from us. But if we think God is behind the trial we won't dare to resist it.

It is true that God uses whatever we face to teach us. But that is not the same thing as God orchestrating evil and causing it. If we respond rightly to God, all the enemy's schemes will be turned and caused to work for our benefit. Our right response is not passive acceptance, but rather active resistance.

God can lead us into situations in which, in order to do His will, we will face attacks from the enemy. Suffering is a part of our Christian walk. Peter comments about this suffering being in the will of God:

1 Peter 4:19
Therefore let those who suffer according to the will of God commit their souls *to Him* in doing good, as to a faithful Creator.

40

Notice that this verse doesn't say anything about God arranging the suffering or our passively accepting it. On the contrary, Peter tells us both the source and the militant attitude we must take toward the source of the suffering.

1 Peter 5:8-9
8 Be sober, be vigilant; because your adversary the devil walks about like a roaring lion, seeking whom he may devour.
9 Resist him, steadfast in the faith, knowing that the same sufferings are experienced by your brotherhood in the world.

Peter tells us that we are to resist Satan who is the author of the sufferings we face. As we press into the will of God, Satan seeks to hinder us from accomplishing our purpose. We are not to passively accept suffering, but rather actively resist the one who is sending it to stop the progress of the Kingdom of God.

The Pressure of Circumstances

The first of the two methods Jesus mentions when discussing the stony ground is tribulation. The word could be translated *pressures of life*. One lexicon gives "to crush, press, compress, squeeze...pressures from evil, affliction, distress." Many of the stressful situations we face are sent by Satan to steal the Word. We are to actively resist and rebuke his influence like Jesus commanded the storm to be still. Not every circumstance will immediately be resolved, but our resisting the devil and his works gets heaven involved in our situations.

Do Trials Develop Our Faith?

Some have suggested that our trials develop our faith. I would suggest that it is not our faith that is developed in our trials, but rather our faith is *tested* in trials. What is developed in our trials is *patience*.

41

James 1:2-3
2 My brethren, count it all joy when you fall into various trials,
3 knowing that **the testing of your faith** produces **patience.**

Trials are sent by the adversary to get the Word out of our hearts. If we resist and overcome him, they work in us something called patience. In our modern usage of this word, we describe something passive, like "just hang in there, it'll all work out." But this Greek word (*hupomone*) is much more dynamic than that. It means "independent, unyielding, defiant perseverance in the face of aggressive misfortune, and thus to a kind of courageousness."[2] Another source calls it the "fortitude of a stouthearted soldier." There is nothing passive about this word.

Don't lie down and take it, stand up and resist it! Call upon God's grace to empower you and then take your stand. Having done all to stand, stand therefore.

Certainly, God works through circumstances and orchestrates them for His purposes. What I am saying is the evil circumstances are sent by the enemy to discourage us and steal the Word. When I first heard this concept of Satan coming through tests and trials, it challenged what I had heard most of my Christian life. I was taught to seek to learn the lesson God was teaching me through my trials.

But when I honestly evaluated the teaching of Jesus in this parable, I had to consider if I had not been mis-taught all my Christian life. If I was going to take anyone's word for it, it ought to be Jesus! He said these trials come to steal the Word and He said it was Satan who wanted to steal the Word.

Jesus said this parable was a foundational parable for all kingdom teaching. If we do not understand this parable, how will we understand any parable, He asked. That is why a proper understanding of what Jesus taught here is so important. So many in the Church are passively accepting what the enemy

---

2 Exegetical Dictionary of the New Testament.

brings into their live to destroy them in the name of submission to God's "dealings." No wonder there is so little victory in the Body of Christ.

Questions

Prayerfully think through this concept of your tests and trials not coming from God. Was Jesus speaking the truth? If so, how does this new perspective adjust your thinking about the circumstances of life? Have you passively accepted evil, thinking you were submitting to God's sovereignty?

I told you this teaching was life-changing for me. This is one of the areas that was forever changed. I have accepted Jesus' teaching in the parable and I no longer accept evil as though it were from God for His mysterious purpose. If it is evil, I resist it. I can not tell you how much more victory I have in my life as a result.

In the next chapter we will look at another method the enemy uses to uproot the Word from our lives.

Chapter Seven

HOSTILITY FROM PEOPLE

Mark 4:17
...and they have no root in themselves, and so endure only for a time. Afterward, when tribulation or **persecution** arises for the word's sake, immediately they stumble.

In the West, we know little about the serious kind of persecution some of our brethren in other countries experience. Some are beaten, imprisoned, scorned or tortured for their faith. We have not been called upon to face this level of persecution.

Yet we face a subtler form of persecution in our culture. The Greek word for *persecution* means *to make to run or flee, put to flight, drive away.*[3] The hostility we find in our culture to our faith is a form of persecution. The suspicious and condescending attitude we face in other believers when we really step out to trust God is also a form of persecution.

Demonic spirits seek to influence others to be hostile to us and challenge us about what we believe. These spirits use the ridiculing and mocking attitude of our society to pressure us out of our promises and make us feel we are stupid to believe in and

---

[3] Thayer's Greek Lexicon, Electronic Database. Copyright © 2000, 2003, 2006 by Biblesoft, Inc. All rights reserved.)

trust God. Traditional Christians will warn us when we attempt to take God at His promises. "That's not for today," they say. They'll admit that God *can* do many powerful things, but they are full of doubt as to His willingness.

That's why the Bible says to "fight the good fight of faith" (1 Tim. 6:12). We fight all the subtle undercurrents of unbelief in our culture and in the Church. We have to "gird up the loins of our minds" (1 Pet. 1:13). We need to stay focused on the promises and protect the incorruptible Seed in our hearts. Persecution and affliction arise because of the Word.

God's Cure

Jesus knows the enemy's tactics. Our trials have the potential of maturing us if we understand and cooperate with our Father. Just as God's cure for the pressure of circumstances was the development of patience, God also has a grace to overcome Satan's attacks through people. This grace is called *longsuffering*.

Ephesians 4:2
...with all lowliness and gentleness, with **longsuffering**, bearing with one another in love...

The love of God in our hearts manifests in longsuffering toward others. If we desire the Word to produce in us, we must cultivate this grace in our lives.

Colossians 3:12
12 Therefore, as the elect of God, holy and beloved, put on tender mercies, kindness, humility, meekness, **longsuffering**...

To guard our hearts against the Word-thief, we must put on longsuffering. The other virtues mentioned in these last two verses are also most practical in protecting the Word from the thief. Becoming longsuffering means we are slow to anger, not quick to retaliate. Longsuffering is also mentioned among the fruit of the Spirit in Galatians 5:22.

When we choose to respond rightly to God in our trials, all that Satan means for evil and his attempts to uproot the Word, ends up working for us and actually develops the virtues of patience and longsuffering. Knowing this, we count it all joy when we find ourselves in trials. We know the trying of our faith is working patience. When patience has its perfect work in us, we will be whole and entire lacking nothing (James 1:2,3).

With this in mind, notice what Paul prays for us:

Colossians 1:9-11
9 For this reason we also, since the day we heard it, do not cease to pray for you, and to ask that you may be filled with the knowledge of His will in all wisdom and spiritual understanding;
10 that you may walk worthy of the Lord, fully pleasing Him, being fruitful in every good work and increasing in the knowledge of God;
11 strengthened with all might, according to the power of His glory, for all **patience** and **longsuffering** with **joy**...

Paul exhorts Timothy in a way applicable to us:

2 Timothy 2:1,3
1 You therefore, my son, be strong in the grace that is in Christ Jesus.
3 You therefore must endure hardship as a good soldier of Jesus Christ.

We all face difficulties and hardships in life. God has made provision for us to get through them in victory and come out of them in better shape than we went in. It all has to do with our learning the right responses to our challenges. We won't change our responses overnight. But with persistence we can develop patience and longsuffering and undermine the enemy's strategy to get the Word out of our lives. The Word can and will bring forth fruit in our lives.

Luke 8:15
But the ones that fell on the good ground are those who, **having heard the word with a noble and good heart, keep it and bear fruit with patience.**

Jesus believes that you have a good and noble heart. He has designed you as a New Creation being conformed to His image to bring forth fruit with patience. Learning to stand on the Word and endure until it brings forth develops your character and makes you strong. Press in and press on!

Chapter Eight

THORNS

As Jesus continues in the parable, he points out other methods
Satan uses to steal the Word before it can bring forth after its
own kind. The incorruptible seed creates the image of Christ in
us and we grow up into Him in all things.

Mark 4:18-19
18 Now these are the ones sown among **thorns**; they are the
ones who hear the word,
19 and the cares of this world, the deceitfulness of riches, and
the desires for other things entering in choke the word, and it
becomes unfruitful.

Thorns also come from seed. Not the incorruptible Seed of
God's Word, but rather the corrupt seed of Satanic lies. When we
seek to implement what we hear, Satan stirs up lies that he
planted in us to choke out the Word. Satan works in our lives and
circumstances in our pre-conversion days to sow many corrupt
seeds that distort our image of God, ourselves and others. When
we are first converted, our minds are largely unrenewed. Satan
uses these unrenewed areas to get a hook in us and manipulate
us.

The Enemy seeks to destroy the family so that our concept of
fatherhood will be distorted. For many in our culture, the image
of father is not a healthy image. We must take notice that Jesus
came to reveal the Father. If you want to know what the Father-

God is like, look at Jesus. He is the perfect representative of the Father. "If you have seen Me, you have seen the Father," He said.

When you think of the Father, do you think of a loving Being who wants to fellowship with you? One who has made every provision for you to come to Him without condemnation? One who has provided His Son's blood to cleanse you of every failure after you became His child? This is who Jesus revealed. Faith - the ability to trust Him unreservedly - flows from His Father heart through the written Word to you. Maintaining your fellowship in a healthy way is the essence of the faith life.

As you discover the "thorns" in your life, challenge them with God's declarative statements. As we learn to abide in the Word, the Truth will set us free.

Jesus lists three of Satan's thorns in these verses. Over the next few chapters we will look at:

- Cares of this world
- Deceitfulness of riches
- Desires for other things

Satan will work, through your flesh, to get you to prioritize the wrong things, even good things, to distract you from the Word you have heard. Let's look at the things Jesus mentions.

Cares of this World

Young's translation puts it "the anxieties of this age." Life is full of challenges. Growing in faith is learning to trust the Lord no matter what we face. Doubt, fear and anxiety are a three-fold weapon to undermine our faith and cause us to doubt God and His Word. What are the anxieties that believers wrestle with?

Our Spiritual Life

First of all, many believers are under the anxious care of their spiritual life. They sense their need to grow and be more Christ-like, but aren't sure how to move forward into growth. Satan harasses them with condemnation about their weaknesses and lack of growth. It needs to be understood that we cannot grow in any area where we are anxious.

Matt 6:27 Webster
Which of you by anxious care can add one cubit to his stature?

Only God can cause you to grow. And He can only do this while we trust Him. So anxiety robs us and hinders our spiritual growth. God can handle you with all your weaknesses. But He needs you to let go of your anxieties and unbelief. You're not too big a problem for God to help you. Cast the care of your spiritual growth over on the Lord.

Our Mind and Emotions

Many of us have needs in our emotional life. Again, you can't fix it. Only the Lord can resolve these issues and bring lasting healing. Commit the areas of struggle to Him in loving trust and ask Him to lead you to the tools that can help you receive healing. You might pray, "Father, I trust You to lead me to all the healing and restoration I need. I give you the care of my unresolved emotional issues. I trust You, Father, and I refuse to carry the burden of my lack of perfection. Your Spirit and Your Word are working in me."

But you can do something about your mind. Many emotional problems are the result of years of wrong thinking. Paul tells us to be transformed by the renewing of our minds. You can take the Word of God that promises victory in the area of your need and attack the stronghold you wrestle with in your life. Persistent declaration of the Truth will uproot and demolish the Lie.

Job 22:28 NASU
You will also decree a thing, and it will be established for you; and light will shine on your ways.

The more you declare the Truth, the more you start to "see" yourself with the answer. Light begins to shine on your path.

Our Bodies

Satan often attacks us with sickness and disease. We can claim the healing that Christ has provided by faith. But we don't control the timing of the manifestation of the healing. We must give the care of the manifestation to the Lord. Our part is to believe we have received. His part is to manifest the healing we have laid hold of by faith.

Fear is actually a "door opener" for demonic spirits that oppress with sickness. It is important to resist all fear of disease strongly. Rebuke the fear and refuse to allow it to torment your mind. Say, "I trust You, Father, with my health. I give You the care of my body. You are helping me."

Our Finances

Money is another area in which we are tempted to fear and worry. Jesus promised us that if we seek first His Kingdom and His Righteousness all the things the world around us is seeking will be added to us (Mt. 6:33). Paul exhorts the Philippians that his God will "meet their needs according to His riches in glory in Christ" (Phil. 4:19). Give your financial cares to the Lord. "Trust in the Lord with all your heart, and lean not to your own understanding" (Prov. 3:5). Guard your heart against financial fears.

51

Our Relationships

As I mentioned earlier in the book, the enemy will use the hostility of people to try to steal the Word. For no apparent reason, people will be upset with us and come against us with anger beyond the norm. To guard our hearts we must learn to humble ourselves, be quick to forgive and not allow (at least to the best of our ability) relationship breakdown. Those closest to us can be used to attack the stand on the Word that we are taking. Don't be surprised by this fact. Satan is ruthless.

Remember, we don't wrestle with flesh and blood. If we look behind the human face of hostility there will often be found a demonic influence. Forgive the human, rebuke the demonic. (Preferably, not to the face of the human!) Don't fall for Satan's trap. He wants you offended. While you are in turmoil, he will steal the Word.

Distracted?

When Jesus warned us about the cares of this world, He used a Greek word that means, "a feeling of apprehension or distress in view of possible danger or misfortune - 'anxiety, worry, anxious concern.'"[4] Another source says "to be drawn in different directions... distraction."[5] All of these cares can bring us into a state of apprehension, distress or distraction. Satan wants to use all these things to accomplish that end.

---

[4] **Greek-English Lexicon Based on Semantic Domain**. Copyright © 1988 United Bible Societies, New York.

[5] **Thayer's Greek Lexicon**, PC Study Bible formatted Electronic Database. Copyright © 2006 by Biblesoft, Inc. All rights reserved.

The Cure

1 Peter 5:6-7
6 Therefore humble yourselves under the mighty hand of God, that He may exalt you in due time,
7 casting all your care upon Him, for He cares for you.

Acknowledge your need of divine help to release your cares to the Lord. Trust His hand to lift them from you. Choose to release them to Him and then receive His care for you. You have the choice between carrying your cares or having His care for you. We can say, "Father, You love me and You care for me. I surrender my cares to You. You can handle them. I let them go. I receive Your care for me. You love me and I can trust You."

Philippians 4:6-7
6 Be anxious for nothing, but in everything by prayer and supplication, with thanksgiving, let your requests be made known to God;
7 and the peace of God, which surpasses all understanding, will guard your hearts and minds through Christ Jesus.

Paul tells us to refuse to be anxious about anything. Pray and ask God to deal with the situation. Thank Him that He has heard your prayer. Receive His peace to guard your heart and mind.

Don't Be Drunk!

Most of us Christians would be shocked if it was suggested we were getting drunk. "That's not acceptable behavior for a Christian" we would protest. Notice what Jesus said about being overcome with care:

Luke 21:34
But take heed to yourselves, lest **your hearts be weighed down** with carousing, drunkenness, and **cares of this life**, and that Day come on you unexpectedly.

Jesus puts having our hearts weighed down with cares in the same class with going to wild parties and getting drunk. He indicates that worry and anxiety can have the same effect on the heart as getting drunk. A drunk person loses their focus, cannot talk intelligently, often can't walk in a balanced way and can be dangerous to themselves and to others. As believers, we can be "drunk" on care and worry.

George Muller once said, "When worry comes in, faith leaves. When faith comes in, worry leaves." We can't do both at once. Let's believe and not worry! Do not let the cares of this life steal the Word.

Chapter Nine

DECEIT!

As we look at the methods of the enemy to steal the Word, we come to another tool in the enemy's tool belt.

Mark 4:19
…and the cares of this world, **the deceitfulness of riches**, and the desires for other things entering in choke the word, and it becomes unfruitful.

Money is a powerful thing in our lives. We must have it to live and much of our time is spent accumulating it. Jesus said we cannot serve money and God simultaneously.

Matthew 6:24
No one can serve two masters; for either he will hate the one and love the other, or else he will be loyal to the one and despise the other. You cannot serve God and mammon.

Money and wealth beckon us to their allegiance. Like a seductive woman, Mammon calls us to serve in her courts. True Bible prosperity begins when we break the grip that Mammon may have on our lives through repentance and development of the grace of giving. Money can be deceiving because it promises us the security that only God has to offer. Men trust in wealth just like they would trust in God.

55

1 Timothy 6:10
For the love of money is a root of all kinds of evil, for which some have strayed from the faith in their greediness, and pierced themselves through with many sorrows.

Observe that this does not say "money is the root of all kinds of evil." It says that the "love of money" is the source of many things that are evil. Money is a useful tool when in the hands of a mature believer who seeks first the Kingdom of God. But the love of money causes us to stray from our faith.

Godly Prosperity

The seductive power of greed is not the only deceitful aspect of Mammon. God's Word teaches that as we seek first the Kingdom of God the things that the world around us is clawing for will be added to us. We should expect God to prosper us and bless the work of our hands (Deut. 28:8). One of the basic laws of the Covenant is increase and multiplication. The secret is to not seek this *first*. We seek first His rule over our lives. He grants the increase.

The idea that Christians should be poor is not Biblical. Christians should not *love money!* Believers are called to bring good news to the poor and to minister to their needs. How can you minister to the poor if you are the poor?!! We should have enough for our own needs and then some to meet the needs of others who don't know our God. (Or, the needs of our brother or sister who find themselves in need). Trust God to develop your character to the place He can trust you with money. He's looking for people who will distribute financial help to others without majoring on their own blessings. He will bless and prosper such ones as this.

2 Corinthians 9:8
And God is able to make all grace abound toward you, that you, always having all sufficiency in all things, may have an abundance for every good work.

There is a grace - an anointing - to cause us to have an abundance. It is so we can give to "every good work" which God shows us to contribute to. Without His blessing and abundance, we are unable to give as He leads.

Wrong Thinking

If we have wrong thinking about money in our lives, when we hear the Word that promises us our destiny, Satan will attack our finances to distract us from the Word. Financial fear and worry are often large strongholds in the lives of believers. This area must move into the realm of faith where we trust God for our finances or the enemy will use it to keep us distracted and our hearts weighed down.

We must make God the Source of our security and not money. This begins with a decision to renounce any trust in Mammon we may have had. As we grow in trust, God leads us in our giving and we find that as we give it is given to us abundantly. Heaven's principles begin to govern our way of thinking about money. Our financial worries begin to fade away into the background. The "thorns" of wrong thinking about money can no longer be used to steal the Word in our lives.

Are there excesses in prosperity teaching? Undoubtedly. Someone has taken every area of Bible truth to an excess. We must be careful to not be so offended by the overemphasis of some, and throw out the healthy teaching in the Word about finances. Satan will use any area of unhealthy doctrine to steal the Word.

Whenever God reemphasizes a Truth that has been obscured by tradition, some will take that Truth into overemphasis. Satan pressures some into this overemphasis in order to get a reaction from other believers. This polarizes parts of the Body and creates 'camps' over the controversial subject: those for it and those against it.

Faith is a good example. Without faith it is impossible to please God (Heb. 11:6), yet with the extremes of some there are those who don't want to hear anything about faith. Even the mention of the subject brings a reaction. The Word that God is trying to bring as a fresh emphasis is rejected - some rally around it and overemphasize it - others don't want to hear anything about it. Satan comes to steal the Word. Instead of honestly seeking God to find out what He wants to say on the subject, we divide over it and Satan successfully steals the Word that God has a purpose in bringing.

Chapter Ten

IN THE MINISTRY OF JESUS

We see the same kind of warfare over the Word in the ministry of Jesus. Jesus as a human walked and lived by faith just as we are called to do. Although I'm sure He enjoyed a level of fellowship with the Father that was unbroken, He still had to trust the Father and resist the enemy. As He walked out His calling by faith, events in which His Father speaks to Him in a dramatic way must have been powerful encouragements to continue His mission. So at His baptism when the Father manifested Himself to Jesus and spoke to Him of His place in the Father's heart, it had to be a powerful incentive to keep on walking out His destined purpose.

> **Matthew 3:16-17**
> 16 When He had been baptized, Jesus came up immediately from the water; and behold, the heavens were opened to Him, and He saw the Spirit of God descending like a dove and alighting upon Him.
> 17 And suddenly a voice came from heaven, saying, **"This is My beloved Son, in whom I am well pleased."**

I believe in the full deity of our Lord Jesus Christ. However, as Philippians 2:5-11 says, He humbled Himself and became a Man. Jesus walked this earth not as deity, but as a human absolutely dependent on His Father. The Word says He grew in wisdom and favor. He would not grow in these things as deity, but would as a human. He truly humbled Himself and became like us.

If this is so, then you can see how powerful this event of His Father's affirmation would have been for Him. Notice, however, Satan's first challenge to Him when he tempted Him:

Matthew 4:2-3
2 And when He had fasted forty days and forty nights, afterward He was hungry.
3 Now when the tempter came to Him, he said, **"If You are the Son of God**, command that these stones become bread."

Satan came immediately to steal the Word that was sown. He challenged what the Father had just spoken to Jesus.

He throws the same fiery dart again in his next temptation...

Matthew 4:6
4 ...and said to Him, **"If You are the Son of God**, throw Yourself down. For it is written:
5 'He shall give His angels charge over you,' and, 'In their hands they shall bear you up,
6 Lest you dash your foot against a stone.'"

Jesus, as a Man, effectively resisted him using the written Word of God to defeat him. We can follow His example in our warfare. Jesus is our example.

Another Example

After Jesus spent much time teaching them about the meaning of this parable and other parables of the Kingdom, He made a statement that, like all His statements, was the will of God for them.

Mark 4:35
On the same day, when evening had come, He said to them,
"Let us cross over to the other side."

Notice that it was on the same day He had expounded the
parable of the sower to them. It was fresh in their hearing. The
Sower had just released a fresh command from the Father. They
got in the boat and headed out.

Mark 4:36-38
36 Now when they had left the multitude, they took Him
along in the boat as He was. And other little boats were also
with Him.
37 And a great windstorm arose, and the waves beat into the
boat, so that it was already filling.
38 But He was in the stern, asleep on a pillow. And they
awoke Him and said to Him, "Teacher, do You not **care** that
we are perishing?"

Satan came immediately with a storm to hinder the
accomplishment of God's will. Looking at the storm, the
disciples were struck with the "cares of this world" and
completely forgot that the Son of God had said, "Let us go over
to the other side." Jesus was in total peace because He had heard
from His Father and had spoken forth what His Father had given
Him. He was not distracted by any storm Satan might throw His
way.
Notice that Jesus didn't get up and say, "Father, what are You
trying to teach us by this storm?" He saw it for what it was:
Satan attempting to hinder the accomplishment of the Father's
purpose.

Mark 4:39-41
39 Then He arose and rebuked the wind, and said to the sea,
"Peace, be still!" And the wind ceased and there was a great
calm.

40 But He said to them, "Why are you so fearful? How is it that you have no faith?"
41 And they feared exceedingly, and said to one another, "Who can this be, that even the wind and the sea obey Him!"

The disciples had been successfully casting out demons and healing the sick. They had been exercising the authority of Christ's anointing. But somehow this hadn't translated into the "unspiritual" affairs of life. Jesus, in this statement, "How is it you have no faith," was not asking them why they didn't have faith in Him, but rather why they did not understand that Satan was behind the storm and rebuke him themselves. Jesus had just explained how things work and they (apparently) applied it to ministry instead of to life in general.

Kingdom principles are designed to work in real life situations. So often, Christians only apply Truth to the "spirit realm." This is the influence of Greek thinking on the Western Church. In other parts of the world, they apply Truth to all of life, which is the Biblical world view. We are learning to change our paradigm as well. All of life is spiritual; therefore Truth applies to all of life.

Satan attempted to steal the Word from the Son of God. He effectively resisted and overcame these attempts. Jesus is our example and we can resist and overcome too.

Hebrews 4:15
For we do not have a High Priest who cannot sympathize with our weaknesses, but was in all points tempted as we are, yet without sin.

Hebrews 12:2
...looking unto Jesus, the author and finisher of our faith, who for the joy that was set before Him endured the cross, despising the shame, and has sat down at the right hand of the throne of God.

Jesus is the Author and Perfecter of our faith. As we look unto Him and to the joy that is set before us (the fruit of the Word in our lives) we can endure all the hardship we face and overcome the world, the flesh and the devil. The Word is bringing forth fruit in us!

Chapter Eleven

THIRTY, SIXTY AND A HUNDREDFOLD

Mark 4:20
But these are the ones sown on good ground, those who hear the word, accept it, and bear fruit: some thirtyfold, some sixty, and some a hundred.

As we have seen in the previous chapters, the spiritual warfare in our lives centers around the place that the Word of God takes in our lives. Stop the Word, stop the growth of the Word. Notice in the above verse that even with the good ground, the Word brings forth in three levels.

Many believers, when they face a new problem, look to the Lord for a new, deeper revelation. In 27 years of pastoring, I find that most don't need a new revelation, they need a deeper revelation of the basics. They need to move from a thirtyfold revelation to a sixtyfold revelation of the same truth. Others need to move from a sixtyfold revelation to a hundredfold revelation. We move from a revelation of forgiveness, to a revelation of righteousness, to a revelation of dominion.

The Word reveals stages of growth in our understanding of Truth and therefore progressive influence of the Word over our life and behavior. Our goal is to grow up into Him who is the Head in all things, being fully conformed to Christ. The Parable of the Sower has application at every stage of growth we face. But are we reaching for the hundredfold stage of Christian living?

For example, you were saved by faith. Receiving Christ as Savior was the first thing you did with your faith. Yet, 1 Cor. 13 tells us that in the end there will abide faith, hope and love. All three things mentioned here will be relevant in our maturity as well. Faith can be strong or weak, growing or stagnant, overwhelmed by unbelief, therefore pleasing or unpleasing to God. We want our faith life to be constantly pleasing to God. So we must feed our faith and keep it healthy. Since faith comes by hearing, and hearing by the Word of God, we must keep feeding ourselves on the Word and stimulating the growth of our faith.

As our faith grows we apprehend and receive more and more of our inheritance in Christ. We develop from "line upon line, precept upon precept." It is important to note that maturity is not climaxed by being "strong, the Word of God abiding in us and our overcoming the evil one" (1 John 2:14). John describes this level as the Young Men stage of development (sixtyfold). The highest level is the Father's stage where we live to invest in others (hundredfold).

The goal of our lives is to be so intimate with the Father through the Word that the Word becomes His living voice to us. We rest in our place in Christ and live to invest in the maturation of others. "Give and it shall be given unto you," Jesus said. As we invest in others, God invests in us. As we promote others, God promotes us.

As we mature, the Parable of the Sower and it's principles become our normal way of thinking. Our minds become renewed to applying these principles to all of life. We become established in the Truth.

My prayer for you is that the message of this book would become Living Seed for you and Satan would be totally unsuccessful in stealing the Word from your heart.

Other Materials by Joe McIntyre

E.W. Kenyon and His Message of Faith: The True Story

Ever wonder what the true roots of the Faith Message were? This book allows E.W. Kenyon, from previously unpublished writings, to answer his critics. Kenyon tells who really influenced him (and who he was opposed to all of his life: the metaphysical cults). This book documents the rich Evangelical history of 19th Century divine healing in what was known as the "Faith-Cure" movement.

Who We Are in Christ

Ever struggle with your identity and sense of worth? Knowing what God has done for you in the Finished Work of Christ will set you free from double-mindedness and establish you in the grace of God. You are a New Creation, the Workmanship of God. God has given you His Righteousness so you can stand in His presence without condemnation. This book is an exposition of these life-changing Truths.

Kingdom Warriors

Rick Joyner, in his Final Quest book, relates a vision in which a horde of demonic forces attack the Church. Many believers cave in to these forces, Joyner points out, because they did not have on their armor. This book is an in-depth look at the armor with practical ways to implement it in daily life. These Truths were personally life-changing for the author.

Many CD sets on a number of subjects, including the Parable of the Sower and War Over the Word, are also available at our website: thehealingcentre.us/wohg, or call 425.424.3801.